Building Marriages
that Last a Lifetime!

Together Forever

God's Design for Marriage

Premarital Mentor's Guide

ED & ANGIE WRIGHT

What others are saying about the premarital mentoring program

Together Forever | God's Design for Marriage

Pastors and churches who marry or minister to couples have a responsibility to do everything they can to ensure the long-term success, survival, and sanctity of the marriage covenant. That is the exact reason why I do not marry a couple unless they have been through *Together Forever* and why our church has installed it as a pillar of pastoral care along with *Putting the "Happily" Into Your Ever After* for already married couples. You simply cannot beat the combination of a trained Marriage by God mentor couple interactively processing the curriculum with a prospective or struggling couple. Every church that wants integrity in its couples or marriage ministry would serve its members and community well by installing Marriage By God.

KENNY LUCK, *Lead Pastor at Crossline Community Church, Award-Winning Author, Founder of Every Man Ministries*

In addition to the *Together Forever: Premarital Mentoring Workbook,* Ed and Angie Wright have enabled you who serve as mentors and disciplers to succeed by following the easy-to-do steps in mentoring. *The Together Forever: Premarital Mentor's Guide* helps you anticipate reactions from the couple you mentor and be prepared and prayed-up to graciously encourage, guide, and respond. This will be a great asset to help you be prepared to contribute to a great marriage in the making.

DR. HAROLD J. SALA, *Founder of Guidelines International, Author*

Practical! That is the word that came to mind as I read Ed and Angie Wright's *Together Forever* premarital mentor's guide. Their easy-to-follow guide helps direct the mentoring couple who wants to assist other couples in maximizing their relationship and avoiding the pitfalls that so easily trip up the new bride and groom. As you read the guide, you'll say to yourself, "I can do that!"

DARLENE SALA, *Author, Seminar Speaker*

As proclaimed in the name of their ministry, Marriage by God, Ed and Angie Wright's *Together Forever* premarital mentoring workbook and mentor's guide are essential for training engaged couples that seek to fulfill God's purpose in their marriage. Their mentor's guide reveals that not many should become teachers because God holds them to a higher standard. The Wrights represent the highest expression of God's intent for married couples and I wholeheartedly endorse without reservation these two excellent books.

WILLIE NAULLS, *Pastor, Author*

Very subtle changes from the earlier version of these materials have taken this mentoring program from good to great! We love it, and the Twenty-One Questions are a great addition to use as a quick reference in fine-tuning a couple's relationship.

HAROLD K. WEBBER, *Pastor of Living Way Christian Fellowship*
CHESTER & CHERYL YOUNG, *Directors of Marriage Enrichment*

Ed and Angie Wright have beautifully put together a guide for both engaged couples as well as mentor couples. The guide is rich with spiritual and practical insights, with the end goal being for the engaged couple to be intentional about their marriage. The Wrights have given the whys behind intentionality as well as the practical tools and steps to make an intentional marriage possible. With humility and grace, the material is presented in a systematic, easy-to-follow weekly format. A fabulous resource in a world that is desperate for such content!

KIM MOELLER, *Christian Author and Speaker*

Ed and Angie Wright have written a beautiful and biblical book on helping premarried couples understand the full beauty of God's plan for marriage. They masterfully weave personal stories and insights to illustrate the elements of a biblical marriage that are completely practical. I highly recommend this resource for those that are mentoring couples considering marriage.

CARL MOELLER, *CEO Biblica - The International Bible Society*

We wish to dedicate this book to the Marriage by God mentor couples who have come beside us with a passion to help couples learn what it looks like to put Christ at the center of their marriage. You have humbly accepted God's assignment, and it has been exciting watching the Holy Spirit work in and through you as you pour blessings into the lives of couples preparing for marriage.

"Older women are to encourage the young women to love their husband, and their children...Likewise urge the young men to have self-control, in all things show yourself to be an example of good deeds, with purity in doctrine."

Titus 2:4-7

Table of Contents

Introduction

PREMARITAL MENTORING OVERVIEW

As iron sharpens iron, so one man sharpens another
— Proverbs 27:17

CONGRATULATIONS ON YOUR DECISION TO BECOME A MENTOR COUPLE to engaged couples. You have been selected because you expressed an interest in the ministry and appear to be living a joy-filled, Christ-centered, long-term marriage (ideally ten years or more).

Marriage is tough. There is no way around it. However, with the proper biblical principles and the loving guidance of Christian mentors, the institution of marriage becomes the rich blessing God intended it to be. This program is designed to show engaged couples how to live out God's design for marriage in order to stay together for a lifetime. Throughout the process, you, as mentors, will share biblical principles and time-tested techniques for fulfilling God's great plan for marriage.

Your goal as a mentor couple is not to solve their problems but to equip them with the tools needed to solve their own problems. As is often said, "Give a man a fish; you feed him for a day. Teach a man to fish, and you feed him for a lifetime."

This program is designed for you to meet with your couple for six sessions to guide them through the materials. In preparation for each session, the engaged couple will read the three chapters that make up each session and answer the corresponding questions. Each one is to complete their homework independently. They will be asked not to share their answers before coming together for their session. This allows for truth and spontaneity to come out during the sessions. It also allows for much more successful, open-minded mentoring sessions.

At each session, you, the mentoring couple, will lead the couple through each chapter as they share their answers. You will be there to encourage, inspire, and affirm the couple in their areas of strength. You will also be there to share with the couple, openly and honestly, the wealth of knowledge and experience gained from your Christ-centered marriage. The notes in your mentor's guide will help you educate the couple on fundamental principles and tools that will aid them in having a solid marriage in Christ. Your job is to be there with guidance to challenge and motivate the couple to make appropriate changes in the areas that need strengthening.

Studies show that the happiest people in the world are married. Unfortunately, studies also show that the unhappiest people in the world are married. As you can see, the stakes are high. When couples learn God's blueprint for marriage, the institution of marriage becomes the rich blessing God intended it to be.

REMEMBER THESE IMPORTANT POINTS WHEN MENTORING A COUPLE

- Be open and honest with your couple and encourage them to be the same.

- Assure your couple that you will keep all information they share confidential.

- Be exceptional listeners.

- Be more interested than interesting. Try to listen at least 70 percent and talk no more than 30 percent. Remember, this is your couple's time to grow together.

- Show them through your facial expressions and eye contact that you are listening and interested in what they are saying.

- Be careful not to express any feelings of judgment or disapproval.

- One of the great values of mentoring couple-to-couple is that men and women sense things differently. So if you intuitively feel there is more to someone's answer than what they've spoken, try to draw out their feelings by saying, "Tell me more," or asking open-ended questions such as, "I sense there is a little more that you have to say on this. Will you elaborate?" This is especially important on topics that are difficult for them to discuss.

- Use statements like, "What do you think about what your fiancé just shared?" or "Explain a little more about what you are trying to say."

- Give loving guidance that is consistent with God's principles and Word.

- Share helpful insights when appropriate.

- Be aware of what your couple is saying, not only through words but also through body language.

You will walk beside your couple, giving them the unconditional love of God by listening, remaining nonjudgmental, and sharing wisdom. Their confidential, open, and trusting relationship with you will allow your couple to talk through important issues in their relationship and even explore areas that the couple may have avoided. Every couple will have problems exposed. Help and encourage them to grow in their areas of weakness or insecurity. Affirm them in their areas of strength.

Although this program is designed to be a "wellness care" program, issues may sometimes be exposed that require extra time and attention. In rare instances, a serious area of concern may reveal itself (abuse, addiction, intense anger, infidelity, etc.). Immediately bring this to the attention of the ministry leader or pastor.

THE GIFT GOES ON

While this program is designed to help engaged couples, there is also an incredible bonus for you, the mentoring couple. Coaching couples will strengthen your own marriage. As you instruct about God's design for marriage, you will grow in your understanding of living a Christ-centered marriage. You will also find yourselves sharing these principles and techniques with others, which will encourage their growth toward having Christ-centered relationships. Ultimately this program will help each couple involved grow in their love for one another and grow deeper in their love for God. They will live out the greatest commandments of all: to love God and love others. That's proof again that you cannot out-give God!

Before You Meet

Review the three chapters in the Together Forever: *God's Design for Marriage: Premarital Mentoring Workbook* that you will be covering tonight with your couple so you are familiar with the session content.

YOUR GOALS FOR THE FIRST SESSION WILL BE TO:

• Get to know your couple and set the stage for open and honest discussion.

• Be a good listener.

• Be alert to your couple's body language, which often communicates more than the words they speak.

• Begin identifying your couple's strengths.

• Begin identifying your couple's areas of needed growth.

Identifying your couple's strengths and desired growth areas will allow you to customize the mentoring program to your couple's needs. When your couple is strong in an area, don't spend too much time on those questions. On the other hand, when your couple exposes an area that needs attention, feel free to give an extra homework assignment to help them grow in that area, or do a deeper dive into the subject.

If you find either one or both individuals giving brief answers to the questions, provide a pregnant pause after they finish. This will hopefully prompt them to expand their response. Don't be afraid to allow for times of silence. Remember, the success of the mentoring is based on their willingness to communicate openly and honestly with each other.

HERE ARE A FEW ADDITIONAL NOTES BEFORE YOU START:

• The questions from the workbook are in bold print.

• Have the woman answer the odd questions first, and have the man answer the even questions first, thus alternating back and forth. They will both answer all the questions.

• The mentor notes are written so that you can, if you like, read the information to your couple. However, we recommend being familiar enough with the material that your discussions flow freely.

Chapter 1

TWO BECOMING ONE

For this reason, a man will leave his father and mother and be united to his wife, and they will become one flesh — Genesis 2:24

---

1. Give at least three advantages to being married over being single.

There are many advantages to being married over being single. Some of the benefits are companionship, emotional support, physical intimacy, the possibility of building a family, and sharing life experiences together. In addition, it is special to have someone on your team, cheering your successes, encouraging you through your challenges, supporting you in your sorrows, and loving you no matter what.

2. What would you like to see God accomplish through this premarital mentoring program? Be specific.

This gives all of us an idea of what you are expecting to accomplish. Do you each agree with what your partner answered?

3. Have you had a breakup anytime since you became exclusive? If so, what was the reason?

It is not uncommon for a couple to break up during their courtship. In fact, it can actually be healthy. A breakup can strengthen your resolve that you cannot see yourself going through life without your fiancé. It can help you work towards strengthening your love and commitment. However, if there have been repeated breakups, this can be evidence that you have some negative relationship patterns that need to be broken for the health of your relationship. We will be sharing numerous skill sets to help you resolve conflicts and differences in a healthy manner.

4. How do you feel about divorce?

Understanding what the Bible says about divorce is essential. Two key verses show us God's attitude towards divorce. First, Malachi 2:16 states, "I hate divorce, says the LORD God of Israel." Second, Matthew 19:6 says, "…so they are no longer two, but one. Therefore what God has joined together, let man not separate."

Although the Bible allows for divorce in certain situations (such as infidelity), divorce should never be considered the best option. Couples should always consider reconciliation as their first option. Couples who consider divorce a viable option consider it more easily when their marriage undergoes stress or becomes unsatisfactory to one or both partners.

❤ DEMONSTRATE THIS ILLUSTRATION FOR YOUR COUPLE:

Do you know why we wear our wedding rings on our fourth finger? Let me share a little illustration with you. Bring your two open hands together. Now, bend your middle fingers at the knuckle and bring them together. Have your remaining fingers all touch tip to tip. As you observe your hands in this manner, your middle fingers represent God at the center of your marriage relationship. Your thumbs represent your parents. Try to pull your thumbs apart. They come apart very easily. This is because we are meant to grow up and leave our parents' household. Our pointer fingers represent our siblings. These fingers also separate easily because our siblings also grow up and leave their parents' house. Our little fingers represent our children. Once again, these fingers separate because our children too are meant to grow up and leave their parents' household. However, when you hold your fingertips together and try to separate your ring fingers, you cannot do it. This is because God intends for marriage to last a lifetime. What God joins together, let no one separate.

Not only should divorce not be an option, but you should also make a pact with each other that you will never threaten divorce to hurt or create an impact.

5. On a scale of 1 to 10, rate your compatibility in the seven areas below.
   1 = not compatible at all   10 = extremely compatible

FACTOR	RATING	FACTOR	RATING
Fun		Forgiveness	
Friendship		Future	
Finance		Faith	
Family			

*Will be going into detail on each of these topics in future chapters.

❤ DO YOU HAVE ANY QUESTIONS ABOUT CHAPTER ONE?

Chapter 2

LOVE SPOKEN HERE

God is love — 1 John 4:8

---

1. Which of the three types of love needs the most growth in your relationship (eros, philia, or agape)?

Keeping all three types of love alive in our relationship is essential. We can easily become lazy or complacent in one or more areas if we're not careful.

The most important thing to a woman is to be cherished by her man. The best way to love her is to show her and others how special she is to you.

A man's greatest desire is to be respected by the woman in his life. The best way to respect your man is to be his biggest fan. This should be done privately and publicly.

2. How often does your fiancé tell you that they love you?

You may not have grown up hearing the words "I love you," and you may be uncomfortable speaking them, but it's vital that you learn to tell your partner frequently that you love them. Keeping the love alive is essential. Take advantage of special moments with your future spouse to give a big hug or an extra-long kiss. Speak the words "I love you" daily. These simple gestures will keep love present in your marriage.

Better yet, a study conducted by the National Communication Association found that hearing "I love you" from your loved ones actually lowers stress.

3. If you were having a bad day, how could you avoid taking it out on your fiancé?

First and foremost, pray. Go to the source of love and ask to be filled with love towards your fiancé even though you might be feeling hurt, angry, or frustrated.

Then, talk with your fiancé in a healthy way. Tell your future spouse what is bothering you; for example, "I missed my dental appointment today" or "I have so much work to catch up on, I feel overwhelmed and frustrated."

Remember that love is not a feeling. It is an act of your will, a choice. You can practice the art of "acting your way into a feeling." This means that even though your day is going badly, act and respond the way you would if you were having one of your best days ever. Eventually, the bad-day feelings will become less significant, and you will probably start having a better day.

Ultimately, remember Ephesians 4:29, which states, "Do not let any unwholesome talk come out of your mouths, but only what is helpful for building others up according to their needs, that it may benefit those who listen."

4. Review the passage on love in 1 Corinthians 13:4–8. Which of the actions described in this passage may be challenging for you to show your fiancé? Why?

The beauty of Christianity is learning to love as God loves. Few situations test this as radically as marriage. It is easy to feel overwhelmed by the Apostle Paul's definition of love. It is impossible to demonstrate perfect love all the time to our partner, but as we receive God's love, we can love our mate with the overflow of God's love. God's love will allow you to communicate love to your fiancé in a consistent, creative, and uninhibited way. The bonus is that others will notice, and God will be honored.

5. List ten things you love about your fiancé.

Keep this list available and refer to it often. You may even want to have it read at your wedding ceremony. Whenever you become discouraged about your relationship, reread the list of things you wrote that you love about your fiancé. One of the most effective tools for overcoming marital disappointment is replacing a negative thought about your husband or wife with a positive thought (such as those on the list of all of the things you love about your partner). Studies show that we can focus on only one emotion at a time: choose love.

 **DO YOU HAVE ANY QUESTIONS ABOUT CHAPTER TWO?**

Chapter 3

THE FREEDOM OF FORGIVENESS

Forgive as the Lord forgave you — Colossians 3:13

---

1. Why is it important to forgive your fiancé?

You need to forgive because forgiveness is foundational to our Christian belief system. God loved us so much that He sent His Son to die for the forgiveness of our sins. God wants us to receive His forgiveness and forgive as He forgave us. Colossians 3:13 tells us, "Bear with each other and forgive whatever grievances you may have against one another. Forgive as the Lord forgave you."

The Greek word for forgive is *charizomai*, which means "to show grace or grant a pardon." Even if you haven't experienced the need to forgive your partner for very much at this point in your relationship, marriage is the union of two imperfect people whose faults will be exposed due to the intimacy of the relationship. A healthy marriage will cultivate the attitude of forgiveness that Christ models.

2. How do you forgive someone you are having trouble forgiving, and how do you know you have forgiven them?

We forgive by faith, out of obedience to God. God wants us to love others and to love Him. This love He speaks of is a choice, not a feeling. We must trust God to complete His work in us. Make it between you and God and not between you and the other person. Turn your heart over to God.

Corrie ten Boom, a Christian who survived a Nazi concentration camp, said, "Forgiveness is the key that unlocks the door of resentment and the handcuffs of hatred. It is a power that breaks the chains of bitterness and the shackles of selfishness."[1]

When you forgive someone, you no longer want to hurt them with your words or actions. You aren't bitter about the issue that hurt you. One of the most loving actions you can continually take is forgiveness.

---

[1] Corrie ten Boom, *Clippings from My Notebook* (Nashville: Thomas Nelson, 1982), pg 19.

3. When you forgive someone, must you also trust them?

Forgiveness and trust are entirely separate. Forgiveness is something you give to another person. Trust is something they must earn. God calls us to forgive those who have wronged us immediately—but this does *not* mean that we must immediately trust them. When a breach of trust requires forgiveness, it may take some additional time for the confidence to be fully restored. Trust is something that must be earned—through consistent accountability and time. As you read in the chapter, Joseph immediately forgave his brothers and even understood the bigger picture that what his brothers had meant for evil, God had used for good. But Joseph tested his brothers before he trusted them.

God wants us to forgive often and freely, but sometimes when trust has been broken, it is appropriate to establish boundaries until trust is earned back. Therefore, understanding the distinction between forgiveness and trust is essential.

4. Which of the mindsets for cultivating a forgiving heart will be most helpful going forward?

5. Is there anyone in your life you need to forgive, or from whom you need forgiveness? What is preventing forgiveness from taking place?

Some find it difficult to forgive; others find it challenging to ask for forgiveness. So, what is standing in the way of your forgiveness issue? When you don't clear up areas of forgiveness in your life, you allow them to occupy negative space in your mind.

Not forgiving is like taking poison, thinking it will hurt the other person. Instead, take your hurting heart to the Lord and ask for His help in forgiving.

Often, healing can be achieved through writing a well-worded letter (be careful not to include negative tag-ons). Sometimes it can be accomplished by simply hugging the person and asking, "Can we start over?" Turn to God, the Author of forgiveness, for your strength and peace. There is freedom in forgiveness!

DO YOU HAVE ANY QUESTIONS ABOUT CHAPTER THREE?

CLOSING COMMENTS

- Ask your couple if they are willing to make a premarital covenant to stay sexually pure until their wedding night. If so, tell them you will help hold them accountable by asking them each week.

- Set up a time for your next session.

- Close in prayer.

Before You Meet

The main emphasis in Session Two is for the couple to understand the importance of putting Christ at the center of their relationship. They will discuss how well they feel their fiancé is fulfilling their needs. Finally, they'll discuss how they view their future marital roles.

Depending on your couple's spiritual maturity, you may ask one (or both) to open your session in prayer. If you detect they may be hesitant or embarrassed, then you or your spouse should take the lead.

HERE ARE SOME ADDITIONAL TIPS:

- Encourage your couple to direct their answers towards each other and not to you. This will allow you to observe their reactions and interactions with each other. If you perceive negative or extreme responses, have each person comment and clarify their thoughts and feelings. Ask them to share what they thought of their partner's answer. Allow discussion to continue as long as the conversation moves in a positive direction. If the discussion leads to a conflict that cannot be resolved at that moment, move on to the next question. Explain that they will learn a process in Session Four that will help them resolve conflict.

- If either individual did not complete all their homework, remind them that completing the homework is crucial to the success of their premarital mentoring experience. In addition, completing their assignment is an indication of their commitment to their marriage.

- During the week, you may wish to email your couple reminders and words of encouragement. The husband should email the man, and the wife should email the woman.

- Each week, it is vital that you read the mentor's notes for each of the three chapters so you understand each question's purpose in the chapter. In addition, you need to be familiar with the chapter content in the couple's workbook for the three chapters you will be covering during the session.

Chapter 4

PUTTING CHRIST AT THE CENTER OF YOUR MARRIAGE

Jesus answered, "I am the way and the truth and the life.
No one comes to the Father except through me" — John 14:6

 ASK YOUR COUPLE IF THEY HAVE BEEN FAITHFUL TO THEIR PREMARITAL COVENANT

1. Have you put Christ at the center of your life? If so, how?

When you put Christ at the center of your life, you allow God to direct all your decisions and actions. It means you have a vibrant, ongoing, daily relationship with God, the Provider of all things. You recognize God as your Creator, Savior, and Lord of your life. It also means that you seek to glorify Him in every aspect of your life—especially in your marriage.

2. HUSBAND-TO-BE ONLY: What does loving your future wife as Christ loved the Church mean to you?

WIFE-TO-BE ONLY: What does submission to your future husband in a Christ-centered marriage mean to you?

MENTOR NOTE

Have the wife-to-be and husband-to-be answer question 1, and then review Appendices 1 and 2 in their workbooks with them. The two appendices begin on the next page for you.

Appendix 1

WHAT IT MEANS TO BE A GODLY HUSBAND

THE BIBLE SAYS THE SPIRIT, WHO IS IN EVERY BELIEVER, PRODUCES ACTS of godliness, "love, joy, peace, patience, kindness, goodness, faithfulness, gentleness, self-control" (Galatians 5:22–23). Godliness involves a genuine striving to imitate Christ, to be like Him in thought and action. These characteristics of a godly disposition apply to every believer, whether male or female. Husbands are given additional instructions on how to be Christlike husbands.

"Husbands, love your wives, just as Christ loved the church and gave Himself up for her…In this same way, husbands ought to love their wives as their own bodies. He who loves his wife loves himself. After all, no one ever hated his own body, but he feeds and cares for it, just as Christ does the church—for we are members of His body." (Ephesians 5:25 & 28-30). In this passage, husbands are being called into a very deep, sacrificial, unconditional love. Christ loved the church so much that, even while we were still sinners, He went to the cross and died for us.

Philippians 2:3-4 says, "Do nothing out of selfish ambition or vain conceit. Rather, in humility, value others above yourselves, not looking to your own interests but each of you to the interests of the others." In marriage, this can be particularly difficult. It may mean you need to forgo watching that big game to attend a family function. It is not easy doing what is most loving when it is different from what you want. We need to remember to consider the feelings and ideas of our wives, rather than assuming they think as we do.

Husbands are also given the role of leadership in the marriage. Godly leadership is not a dictatorship. This does not mean that a husband controls all areas of marriage. Instead, a godly leader recognizes who has the best giftedness in given areas and gives jurisdiction for those responsibilities to the best-qualified person.

SPIRITUAL LEADERSHIP

God holds men responsible for the spiritual and physical well-being of their families. Therefore, an ongoing personal relationship with Jesus is crucial when leading a family spiritually. Here are some specific ways you can be an effective spiritual leader of the family.

PRAY FOR YOUR WIFE AND FAMILY

Have a disciplined set time that you pray daily. Also, pray randomly, especially when special needs arise.

PRAY TOGETHER WITH YOUR WIFE

Have a disciplined set time that you pray together with your wife. Many couples pray in bed together every day. Praying with and for your wife at the end of the day can be some of the best foreplay. If you have children, praying together as a family at least once a week will bond you in a special way. When our kids were still at home, we used to meet twenty minutes before we would normally leave for church each week to pray as a family. If you regularly pray together, it will be natural to pray together when special needs arise.

ATTEND CHURCH REGULARLY

Many Christians will attend church when it is convenient. Make attending church as a family a priority.

SPEND TIME IN GOD'S WORD

Regular Bible reading is an important way to help us understand how better to surrender our lives to the Lordship of Jesus Christ. This is also how God can talk to us. A more thorough understanding of the Bible gives us a more Christlike worldview.

JOIN A COUPLE'S SMALL GROUP

A meaningful way to grow in our Christian walk is to fellowship with other believers. Joining a small group will allow you to do life with others who share your values.

GIVE YOUR TIME, TALENTS, AND TREASURES TO GOD

A great way to give your time and talents is to get involved in a ministry. For example, when Angie and I got involved in the premarital mentoring program at church, we did it to give back to God. Little did we know that God was going to pour out blessings on us. In Malachi 3:10, God asks us to test Him. "'Bring the whole tithe into the storehouse, that there may be food in My house. Test me in this,' 'says the Lord Almighty,' 'and see if I will not throw open the floodgates of heaven and pour out so much blessing that there will not be room enough to store it.'" That is a great promise.

MAKE GODLY DECISIONS

Big decisions require God at the center. When you have a decision to make, pray about it, see what the Bible has to say about it, listen carefully to what your wife has to say about it, seek the counsel of Christian mentors, and then make your decision.

BE TENDER TOWARDS YOUR WIFE

The Bible also says, "Husbands, love your wives and do not be harsh with them" (Colossians 3:19). Men have deeper, stronger voices that can sound harsh and intimidating to their wives. It is valuable to understand this and use a loving tone with your wife.

First Peter 3:7 says, "Husbands, in the same way be considerate as you live with your wives, and treat them with respect as the weaker partner and as heirs with you of the gracious gift of life, so that nothing will hinder your prayers." Within the context of this verse, "weaker" does not mean that the wife is in any way "less than" her husband; it means that a woman is not to be treated as "one of the guys." A wise husband will be understanding of this and be sensitive to the differences. A wife desires to be treasured and cherished by her husband.

As you enter marriage, your first ministry is to love and lead your wife. When a husband is consistent in the spiritual leadership of his marriage, it is natural for his wife to respect and follow his lead.

WHAT IT MEANS TO BE A SUBMISSIVE WIFE

THE BIBLE SAYS THE SPIRIT, WHO IS IN EVERY BELIEVER, PRODUCES ACTS of godliness, "love, joy, peace, patience, kindness, goodness, faithfulness, gentleness, self-control" (Galatians 5:22–23). Godliness involves a genuine striving to imitate Christ, to be like Him in thought and action. These characteristics of a godly disposition apply to every believer, whether male or female. The Bible gives even more specific qualifications about what a godly wife looks like.

Proverbs 31 gives a beautiful word picture of a godly wife. Her husband has complete trust in her. The passage describes her as being devoted, dignified, wise, hard-working, and industrious. She takes care of her household. She takes care of herself. She cares for the poor. But, most of all, she loves the Lord and maintains an attitude of joy.

Ephesians 5:21-24 further tells how wives are to conduct themselves, "Submit to one another out of reverence for Christ. Wives, submit yourselves to your own husbands as you do to the Lord. For the husband is the head of the wife as Christ is the head of the church, His body, of which He is the Savior. Now as the church submits to Christ, so also wives should submit to their husbands in everything."

Ultimately, when a wife submits to her husband, she does it out of obedience to God. Jesus (who is co-equal and co-eternal with God the Father and the Holy Spirit) modeled submission to us by perfectly doing the will of God the Father in everything He said and did on earth. A wife should follow this example by worshipfully surrendering her life to Christ by:

- Following her husband's leadership

- Respecting and trusting her husband's opinion

- Seeking her husband's counsel when making decisions

- Believing in her husband's ability to succeed in his areas of responsibility

- Being her husband's helpmate

- Honoring her husband by talking about him in a positive way

- Praising, affirming, and appreciating her husband

- Being a team player

- Being her husband's No. 1 fan!

- Serving her husband with sacrificial love

- Avoiding nonbiblical criticism or nagging

- Not comparing him unfavorably to others

- Be sensitive that your words are not blaming or controlling him

- Avoid correcting him in front of others

For a wife to be submissive to her husband as Christ was submissive to the Father means she willingly allows her husband to lead. A wife will ultimately answer to God for how well she submits to her husband's leadership whether he is making good, loving decisions or not. Likewise, her husband will answer to God for how well he leads and loves her. However, a wife should not follow her husband into sinful behavior, for God is her ultimate authority.

When a wife is not happy with the direction her husband is leading, she should take her frustrations to God with an open teachable spirit. God may be doing work inside of her through her obedience to submit. God may be protecting her through her husband's direction over what she feels is best. God may want her to lovingly share her thoughts with her husband on why they should follow a different path. God may want to work on her husband's heart while she submits her desires to the Lord. God does not need her to be the Holy Spirit or a "holy nag." God wants her to trust him to meet her needs and give her the proper response.

God ultimately wants you to operate together as one with your husband. Therefore, pray for God to either change your husband's mind or change your heart. In doing this, instead of requiring perfect behavior from two imperfect people, you are looking for the ideal protection and guidance from our perfect God.

As you grow more intimate in your relationship with Christ, you will grow increasingly godly in your marriage.

3. Describe the kind of prayer life you want to have together when you get married.

Ideally, you should pray these four ways:

• Individually at set times

• Individually spontaneously

• Together at set times

• Together spontaneously

If you are not comfortable praying together, perhaps you could start by committing to praying together for a few minutes every week before you go to church. Try to incorporate these elements into your prayer: praising, asking, repenting, and thanksgiving.

Most people view sex as the most intimate interaction between a husband and wife, but truly, prayer is the most intimate communion. In sex, you bare your body, but in prayer, you bare your soul. It doesn't get more personal than that!

Prayer is the most critical component to ensure that your love will last a lifetime.

4. How can your fiancé be praying for you right now?

Regularly asking your partner how to pray for them is a great habit. Sometimes people have a hard time asking for prayer. If you genuinely want to come together as one, then you need to share your heart's desires with your future spouse. This is important to the intimacy of your relationship.

5. How often do you read the Bible?

You have probably heard the quote: "The truth shall set you free." However, this verse is not complete without the prior statement. "If you hold to my teaching, you are really my disciples. Then you will know the truth, and the truth will set you free" (John 8:31-32). We cannot know God's freedom and His will without understanding and obeying His teaching.

6. What sin in your life right now is keeping you from being closer to God?

Many Christians have a "sin of choice" that they can justify. They live a "mostly" sin-free life except for the one sin for which they are willing to give themselves a mulligan. If we want God's best, we need to confess our sin and be willing to turn away from it.

Mentors note: Ask each one if this is how they would answer the question for their partner. Is there anything more that they would identify?

If your couple is currently living together or being sexually active, challenge them to turn away from this sin and save it as the blessing God wants it to be in marriage.

7. What are ten things in your life for which you are thankful?

An attitude of gratitude is one of the most important elements for growing in our faith and our personal relationship with the Lord. The secret to joy is to see God in all our circumstances. God wants us to see His goodness during our happy times and our troubles.

8. If you and your fiancé have a significant decision, what process would you use to ensure you will make a God-honoring decision?

If you have a clear-cut process for making big decisions, you will be able to default to it in times of stress more naturally. It should include:

- Praying to understand God's will (remember, God should be the pilot, not the copilot when making a decision)
- Reading the Bible to get direction
- Discussing it thoroughly as a couple
- Seeking the advice of Christians you respect

If you are still struggling to come together on a decision, remember, God ultimately wants you to operate as one with your fiancé. One exercise that can help is to take a sheet of paper and draw a line down the center of the page. On one side, write the reasons for proceeding. On the other side, site the reasons for not proceeding. Each morning take out the paper and review what you have written. Pray for God to either change your fiancé's mind or change your heart. Ultimately, make a joint decision and don't look back or second guess your decision. Never play the "what-if" or "if only" game.

God wants to be involved in every aspect of our lives, especially our big decisions. Pray for God to give you oneness of heart and peace in your decision. Be sensitive to His leading. In doing this, instead of requiring perfect behavior from two imperfect people, you are looking for the perfect protection and guidance from our perfect God.

 DO YOU HAVE ANY QUESTIONS ABOUT CHAPTER FOUR?

Chapter 5

DEVELOPING AN INTENTIONAL MARRIAGE

The LORD will guide you always; He will satisfy your needs — Isaiah 58:11

---

1. On a scale of 1-10 (10 being the best), to what extent does your fiancé currently meet your needs in each of the following areas?

NEED	RATING
Admiration towards you	
Affection towards you	
Conversational needs	
Family connectedness	
Financial security	
Honesty and openness	
Help with chores or errands	
Recreational activities together	
Maintaining attractiveness	

These are needs generally identified as being important to couples in marriage; however, there is usually a difference in which areas are most important to men and women in marriage.

2. How can your fiancé be more intentional about meeting the needs you outlined above?

3. What are some of the desires for your future marriage that your fiancé may not be aware of?

Some desires you may have are a weekly date night; time to talk about light topics; fun together doing a hobby; cuddle time; transparency with the finances; home-cooked meals; staying physically fit; entertaining with family and friends; hearing affirming statements; having intimate, open, honest conversations; etc.

4. If your partner doesn't meet your expectations and needs, how should you respond?

There will be times when you should share your unmet expectations and needs with your fiancé so that they can be better about meeting them. However, there will be other times in your relationship when it will be more effective to take the focus off your partner meeting your needs and put it onto God. Philippians 4:19 assures us, "God will meet all your needs according to His glorious riches in Christ Jesus." Remember that God promises to meet our needs, not our greed. This concept is explained excellently in the book *Love Focused* by Bob and Judy Hughes.

A key factor to happiness in life is to lower our expectations of others. Conversely, having high expectations of others will lead to a frustrating life of unmet expectations.

As you enter marriage, if you increase what you do for your partner and take the focus off what you expect from them, you will be much happier in your marriage.

We should not hold our fiancé or anyone else responsible for making us happy. Instead, our joy should be found primarily in the Lord. God promises that we will be filled with His joy if we follow His commands. "These things I have spoken to you, that my joy may be in you, and that your joy may be full" (John 15:11).

5. List 5 steps can you take to assure you live an intentional marriage.

The best way to approach having an intentional marriage is always to be thinking of things you can do to improve your relationship without expecting anything in return. Ask yourself every day, "What can I do today to make this the best day possible for my partner?"

Three essential things to keep consistent are regularly praying together, keeping fun alive in your relationship, and having meaningful conversations.

6. If, one day, your fiancé says, "You are going to be king/queen for the day. Give me a list of 5 special things I can do for you today," what items would you list? Also, what day of the week would you like your king/queen day to be?

This is a fun exercise we highly encourage you to incorporate into your relationship each week. Even if your relationship gets a little offtrack, you know there are two days in the week that will help you reset and get back on track.

You may ask your fiancé to give you a foot massage, go with you to a favorite restaurant, take a walk with you, read the Bible with you, wash the car, or go with you to the movies. Be creative—the sky is the limit!

Some weeks may be incredibly hectic. That is okay. Still, try to do a little something that lets your fiancé know they are special to you. Every week does not need to be heroic. It just needs to become an essential part of being intentional in your marriage.

 **DO YOU HAVE ANY QUESTIONS ABOUT CHAPTER FIVE?**

Chapter 6

FINDING THE SWEET SPOT
IN YOUR RELATIONSHIP

And there will be harmony between the two — Zechariah 6:13

---

1. How would you define the sweet spot in your relationship, and when do you know you are in it?

The sweet spot is when you and your fiancé feel connected in all areas—emotional, physical, spiritual, and social. Everything is flowing in a positive way. Interaction is pleasant, happy, kind, and loving. There is harmony in the relationship, and you are feeling oneness.

The opposite of the sweet spot is the sour patch. When you are not connecting emotionally, physically, spiritually, and socially, you have drifted into the sour patch. When you are in the sour patch, you are no longer experiencing oneness. Satan's favorite attack on marriage is to destroy oneness.

You take things the right way when you are in your sweet spot. But conversely, when you are in the sour patch, you often take things the wrong way, and even minor disagreements get blown out of proportion.

Dwelling in the sweet spot in your relationship will draw you together in a lasting and intimate way that grows stronger every year. In this way, you can experience the promise of two becoming one, as expressed in Genesis 2:24. You will experience the joy and contentment that God has planned for you in marriage.

2. You will be asked by your mentors to give a recap of the tools outlined in this chapter. Which tools mentioned are you most likely to use?

MENTOR NOTE

The couples have been asked to review the tools that begin on the next page and to come prepared to share their understanding about them. Ask your couple to close their books. Have the woman explain the odd-numbered skills, and the man explain the even-numbered skills. Make sure they both have a clear understanding of all of them.

TOOLS FOR STAYING IN THE SWEET SPOT

1. PRAYER

When a couple has drifted into the sour patch and humbly comes before God together in prayer, they are more receptive to setting aside their individual agendas and selfish desires. Instead, they are open to seeking the will of God, who loves them and wants them to operate as one. Imagine how healing it would be to pray as a couple when things start to enter the sour patch. This is an excellent step for the man to initiate as the spiritual leader of the family, although a woman can always suggest praying together, too.

2. "I'M SORRY. I WIN!"

Use this tactic to take advantage of your competitive nature and make a game out of forgiving quickly. Whoever says they are sorry first wins! Now instead of letting little things fester, if one of you will promptly say sorry (knowing they just won), you can move forward with a smile. It's a great way to solve a problem and win at the same time. For example, one day Angie and I (Ed) had cross words just as I was getting ready to leave for a meeting. Just after I left the house, I received a text from Angie that read, "I'm sorry." A few seconds later, I received a second text that read, "I win!" It made me laugh, and we were quickly back in our sweet spot.

3. FUN

For the health of your relationship, it is essential to keep fun alive, but this is an area that will disappear when you are in the sour patch. Even if you are not feeling it, plan something fun that you both will enjoy doing together. The simpler, the better. Some couples like going back to doing something they enjoyed when they first dated. Couples should be able to bring out the playful child in each other. Laughter should flow freely. It has been said that fun is the litmus test for a good relationship. Good marriages have fun, and marriages that have fun are good.

4. MAD FOR FIVE MINUTES

There are times that you would like to let your fiancé know that you are a bit upset, but you don't want to make a mountain out of a molehill. An effective way to communicate your displeasure to your fiancé and still keep things in perspective is to say, "I am going to be mad at you for five minutes." You both may laugh at the comment, but the point will have been made.

5. ACT OF KINDNESS

Doing a loving act of kindness towards your fiancé when you are not feeling it is a great way to let your partner know how committed you are to getting back into the sweet spot.

6. LOVE GRAFFITI ON THE MIRROR

Use a dry-erase marker to write a love note to your fiancé. Keep an assortment of dry erase markers in your bathroom so you can be creative with your messages.

7. "HOW FULL IS YOUR LOVE TANK?"

Ask your fiancé, "On a scale of one to ten, how full is your love tank right now?" Follow up by asking, "What would it take to make it a ten?" (This one is perfect for guys because it comes with instructions).

8. REPLACE A CRITICISM WITH AN AFFIRMATION

When you are tempted to criticize your fiancé, stop yourself and replace the critique with a genuine compliment. Criticism is one of the quickest ways to drive your relationship into the sour patch. By praising your fiancé, instead of making the situation worse, you'll make it better.

9. SMILE

A simple smile can change the entire chemistry between you and your partner. A smile will warm the heart of your fiancé. A smile makes you appear more attractive. Studies have shown that smiling reduces blood pressure, lowers stress, boosts your immune system, releases endorphins, makes you more positive, and builds confidence. Smiles are contagious, so be the initiator.

10. TEN THINGS I LOVE ABOUT YOU

In your first session, you each made a list of "Ten Things I Love About You." When you are drifting into the sour patch, pull these lists out and reread what you love about your spouse and what they love about you. Then, once your heart is softened, ask your fiancé to do the same. Now, each of you should add some new items to your list.

11. BIG PICTURE

When you and your fiancé argue, ask yourself, "In the scope of eternity, does this really matter? For the sake of our relationship, can I just let it go?"

12. TEXT

Sometimes a loving text is all it takes to get back into the sweet spot. Recently Angie's phone was nearing the memory limit, and she asked me to help her free some memory. So, I asked her if I could delete her text messages for the last two years. She said, "Yes, all except yours." She explained that occasionally she likes to go back and reread my loving text messages.

13. KING/QUEEN FOR THE DAY

You learned this in an earlier chapter. Hopefully, this is something you will incorporate into your weekly calendar. This is a relationship game changer. It brings your relationship into the sweet spot.

14. SPECIAL TIME

Special time is one-to-one connected time together. It is important to keep dating even after you get married. It doesn't have to be fancy or expensive. It just needs to be kept a priority.

15. "I LOVE YOU"

These words can be music to your partner's ears. Add a hug and a long romantic kiss for extra credit.

16. START ALL OVER

Occasionally you have a day that seems to go sideways from the start. When this happens, all it takes is for one of you to say, "Can we start over?" By prior mutual agreement, this is a pact to start over with no talk of what may have caused the day to go wrong in the first place. This cannot be used for significant problems but is an excellent tool for minor issues.

17. LOVE AND RESPECT

Women want to be cherished by their husbands, and men want to be respected by their wives. So, when you are married, continually do things to make your wife feel special and adored by you (especially in front of others). Let her know you are her protector and will keep her safe and secure. As a wife, continually show your husband you are on his team and his biggest fan. Believe in him and avoid questioning or correcting him in front of others.

18. MAKE IT BETWEEN YOU AND GOD

Make it between you and God instead of you and your spouse. Do the right thing because you want to be pleasing to God, even if you are not feeling it towards your fiancé at that moment.

19. GO OUT FOR ICE CREAM!

 SHARE THIS ILLUSTRATION WITH YOUR COUPLE

A relationship never stays the same: it either gets better or bitter. The words *better* and *bitter* differ only in whether the first vowel is an "e" or an "i." An easy way to remember how a relationship becomes *bitter* is by emphasizing that the "i" in bitter indicates a self-centered relationship. An easy way to remember how to make your relationship better is by emphasizing the "e" in *better* is for Emmanuel which means "God is with us." To sum up, a Christ-centered (better) marriage is a lifelong commitment that requires a vital connection with Christ.

The stresses of life may challenge or even discourage you at times, but there is no reason for your relationship to drift into the sour patch for very long. Instead, be committed to using some of the skills outlined here and developing some of your own to get back into the sweet spot quickly.

A great thought to remember is, *I have suffered a great many catastrophes in my life, most of which never happened.*

3. Share a memory of the two of you having fun together.

Fun is the litmus test of a good marriage. If you are having fun together, your relationship is doing well. Conversely, if your relationship is not doing well, you will find that you are no longer having fun together. As you recall your favorite memories together, you may notice that these moments did not necessarily cost a lot of money. Usually, they are more about the connectedness you are feeling with each other at the time. You are in the sweet spot!

If you are ever struggling with having fun together, try watching blooper videos of your favorite sitcoms. You will end up laughing together, and laughter is such a bonding and healing gift.

DO YOU HAVE ANY QUESTIONS ABOUT CHAPTER SIX?

CLOSING COMMENTS

- Set up a time for your next session.

- Ask your couple to pray together during the following week.

- Close in prayer.

Before You Meet

Depending on your couple's spiritual maturity, you may want to ask one (or both) to open your session in prayer. If you detect they may be hesitant or embarrassed, then you or your spouse should take the lead.

HERE ARE SOME ADDITIONAL TIPS:

• One of the great values of mentoring couple-to-couple is that men and women sense things differently. If you intuitively feel there is more to someone's answer than what they've spoken, try to draw out their feelings by saying, "Tell me more," or asking open-ended questions such as, "I sense there is a little more that you have to say on this. Will you elaborate?" This is especially important on topics that are difficult for them to discuss. You can also use statements like, "What do you think about what your partner just shared?" or "Explain a little more about what you are trying to say."

• If you can see areas of growth that need a little extra work, don't hesitate to give them additional homework assignments that help them grow in these areas. Examples might be to pray together as a couple, encourage each other throughout the week in a challenging area, or find a new way to speak in each other's love language.

• Each week it is vital that you read the mentor's notes for each of the three chapters so you understand each question's purpose in the chapter. In addition, you need to be familiar with the chapter content in the couple's workbook for the three chapters you will be covering during the session.

Chapter 7

PERSONALITY DIFFERENCES

I praise you because I am fearfully and wonderfully made — Psalm 139:14

 ASK YOUR COUPLE IF THEY HAVE BEEN FAITHFUL TO THEIR PREMARITAL COVENANT.

 ASK YOUR COUPLE IF THEY PRAYED TOGETHER THIS WEEK.

ASK YOUR COUPLE IF THEY COMPLETED THE KING/QUEEN FOR THE DAY ASSIGNMENT THIS WEEK.

1. Do you believe you and your fiancé are compatible? Explain.

A great marriage is not based on marrying someone compatible because God does not make any two people perfectly compatible; it is based on learning how to deal effectively with your incompatibilities.

2. The statements below reflect personality traits. On a scale of 1 to 10, describe how well the statement applies to you.
   1 = does not describe at all   10 = very accurately describes me

As your couple rates themselves on the statements below, watch for significant differences and have them discuss those differences. Remind them these are just possible differences. There is no right or wrong to them.

	NEED	RATING
A	I prefer to think things through carefully before moving in new directions.	
B	I enjoy being recognized publicly for my achievements.	
C	I generally don't like change.	
D	I have a daily to-do list and try to complete it.	
E	I am very spontaneous.	
F	I am very neat and tidy. I like things in their place.	
G	I am rarely late to an appointment, meeting, or event.	
H	I feel a sense of accomplishment when I complete a project. I am reluctant to start new projects until the ones I am working on are finished.	
I	I prefer socializing in small groups (ideally with just one other couple) rather than at big parties.	

DO YOU HAVE ANY QUESTIONS ON CHAPTER SEVEN?

Chapter 8

DIFFERENCES BETWEEN MEN AND WOMEN

So God created man in His own image, in the image of God He created him;
male and female He created them — Genesis 1:27

---

1. How do you believe the general differences between men and women will affect your decision-making process in marriage?

You should recognize the unique point of view that each can bring to the discussion. Because women use both sides of their brains simultaneously, they usually weigh the emotional ramifications involved in any decision. They tend to be more relational, sensitive, intuitive, and compassionate. A woman should be aware that she needs to look at some decisions more logically and suppress the emotional side; conversely, since a man typically looks at a situation with logic and not emotion, he should value the emotional aspects that his wife brings into decisions.

Men tend to operate more dominantly out of one side of the brain or the other. When a man becomes very emotional, he may no longer view things in his typical logical manner. When this occurs, it is best if a wife does not push to resolve the issue right then. If you try to present the logical way to view things at this time, it will likely escalate emotions. Let some time elapse, and then revisit the issue. When you understand these differences, you will appreciate how men and women complement each other and can work together to make better decisions.

2. Men and women arrive at their self-esteem in different ways. Taking this into consideration, how can you help strengthen your partner's self-esteem?

To the woman: A man generally gets his self-esteem from his career and by providing for his family. You should be sensitive to this by believing in your man, being interested in his career, appreciating his efforts, and respecting him, especially in public. In short, you need to be your man's **No. 1 fan**!

To the man: A woman generally gets her self-esteem from her relationships. The most important relationship is you. You should be sensitive to this critical role in your fiancée's life, affirm her, appreciate her, and build her up daily. Let her know you want to protect her and keep her safe. Communicate to her how **special she is to you** and that you cherish her!

Everyone should ultimately receive their self-esteem from God. A strong sense of who we are in Christ minimizes our need to draw on our partner so heavily to build our self-esteem.

3. Men and women sometimes have different conversational needs. Has this created a problem in your relationship? If so, how? What solutions do you suggest?

You likely have different needs for sharing, so it is caring for each of you to be sensitive to the other. For example, women tend to give more detail when talking, which can frustrate a man. Women can feel as though their thoughts and ideas are being dismissed, thus making them feel devalued in the eyes of their partner. Women should be sensitive to this and try to bottom-line their conversation, while men should be sensitive to genuinely listening and validating their mate's input.

You should make a priority of having time together each day to communicate. You may need some downtime when you first arrive home from work before diving into extensive conversation. It is also best to avoid talking about serious issues when hungry or tired. Ultimately, there should be some prime time reserved each day for you to come together in meaningful conversation.

Although both men and women benefit by having same-sex friendships, it significantly helps women, who typically have greater relational needs. A wife should seek out God-honoring relationships with other women. Don't use these relationships as a place to complain about your husband, but rather to learn to be a better wife (and, perhaps down the road, a better mother, too).

4. Although men and women do not think alike, seeing things from your partner's perspective will help strengthen your relationship and create better teamwork. What are some ways you can suggest for learning and understanding what is important to your fiancé?

First and foremost, ask your partner to share what is important to them. When you do this, reflective listening is a great tool to make sure you are grasping what they are sharing. After your fiancé shares their thoughts, reflective listening involves you restating what you understood them to say so they can clarify any misunderstanding.

A second way to ensure that your partner comprehends what you are trying to communicate is to use a word picture that is relatable to them so that they can emotionally connect.

 **DO YOU HAVE ANY QUESTIONS ABOUT CHAPTER EIGHT?**

Chapter 9

LOVE LANGUAGES

Above all, love each other deeply, because love covers over a multitude of sins
— 1 Peter 4:8

PLEASE SHARE THE RESULTS OF "THE FIVE LOVE LANGUAGES" TESTS, WHICH CAN BE FOUND IN YOUR WORKBOOK IN APPENDIX 3 FOR WOMEN AND APPENDIX 4 FOR MEN.

IF YOU LOOK AT THE "LOVE LANGUAGES GUIDE" IN APPENDIX 5 IN YOUR WORKBOOK, YOU WILL SEE BASIC ACTIONS TO TAKE AND AVOID FOR EACH LOVE LANGUAGE.

MENTOR NOTE

Appendix 5 from the workbook appears on the next page.

Appendix 5

LOVE LANGUAGES GUIDE

LOVE LANGUAGE	ACTIONS	AVOID
WORDS OF AFFIRMATION	• Compliments • Notes and cards • Kind words	• Criticism
QUALITY TIME	• One-to-one time • Face-to-face interaction • Taking long walks together • Doing activities together	• Allowing other people or priorities to interrupt our special time together
RECEIVING GIFTS	• Giving gifts on special and not-so-special days • More about the thoughtfulness of the gift than the expense of the gift	• Ignoring or forgetting special days
ACTS OF SERVICE	• Helping with chores • Saying things like, "How can I help you?"	• Helping others and not being there for your spouse
PHYSICAL TOUCH	• Touches • Hugs & cuddling • Kisses	• Negative touch

*Chart based on Gary Chapman's book, *The 5 Love Languages*®.

When you understand the concept of speaking in the five different love languages, you will enhance all your relationships. You can learn the love languages of those closest to you and relate in the most meaningful way to them. You can access the love language assessment for free online.

1. On a scale of 1 to 10, how full is your love tank?

2. What could your fiancé do to raise it to a 10?

3. Complete this sentence, "I feel most loved when ..."

Use the three questions above to occasionally test how well you are meeting each other's needs and to know how you can better meet those needs.

 DO YOU HAVE ANY QUESTIONS ABOUT CHAPTER NINE?

 **CLOSING COMMENTS**

- Next week we will discuss families, so please be prepared to share some pictures of your families. Pictures on your phone are fine.

- As additional homework, remind your couple to go to www.marriagebygod.org and watch the *Conflict Resolution Video* under the Resources tab, before the next session. They can watch it together or separately.

- Set up a time for your next session.

- Close in prayer.

Before You Meet

This is perhaps one of the most important sessions you will have with your couple. If this session is successful, your couple will be able to establish a meaningful connection and appropriate boundaries with their extended family, gain new communication skills, and be equipped with a method to assist them in resolving their conflicts. Wow! What a difference you will be making in their lives.

HERE ARE SOME ADDITIONAL TIPS:

- Most sessions are designed to last about an hour and a half. This session may last longer, so pace yourself and focus on what is most important. Quickly move to the next question if you see that your couple is strong in that area.

- Be aware of what your couple is saying during your session, not only through words but also through body language. By now, they should be placing Christ at the center of their relationship and creating a practice of praying together. If they are not doing so, then nicely but firmly, hold them accountable. The husband should keep the man accountable, and the wife should hold the woman accountable.

- In this session, your couple will be introduced to "Ten Steps to Resolve Conflict" and this will be a valuable tool for their relationship. Hopefully your couple viewed the online video dramatization of a couple working through conflict; this is located on the website at http://marriagebygod.org under the Resources tab. If they have an actual conflict to work through, ask them to do it as an extra homework assignment and share the results with you when you meet for your next session.

- Each week it is important that you read the mentor's notes for each of the three chapters so you understand each question's purpose in the chapter. In addition, you need to be familiar with the chapter content in the couple's workbook for the three chapters you will be covering during the session.

Chapter 10

EXTENDED FAMILY

You shall rejoice in all the good things the LORD your God has given to you
and your household — Deuteronomy 26:11

 ASK YOUR COUPLE IF THEY HAVE BEEN FAITHFUL TO THEIR PREMARITAL COVENANT.

 ASK YOUR COUPLE IF THEY PRAYED TOGETHER THIS PAST WEEK.

 ASK YOUR COUPLE IF THEY COMPLETED THE KING/QUEEN FOR THE DAY ASSIGNMENT THIS PAST WEEK.

 DID YOU BRING A PICTURE OF YOUR FAMILY TO SHARE?

1. Genesis 2:24, "Therefore a man shall leave his father and mother and be joined to his wife, and they shall become one flesh." What does this statement mean to you?

As you come together in marriage, the two of you become your own primary family unit. Of course, you should still show love and respect to your extended family, but you have the highest loyalty and devotion to one another.

2. Describe the relationship you have with your parents. How has this relationship shaped or impacted your view of marriage?

Whether we like it or not, our relationship with our parents and what was modeled to us growing up impacts our relationship with our spouse. We either live what we learned (sometimes without realizing it) or intentionally choose to live differently. Sometimes we transfer emotional needs that were not appropriately met by our parents into our marriage in an unhealthy way—acknowledging how these parts of our history play into our marriage leads to new healthier patterns.

3. Do you ever share relationship problems with a family member?

Vigilantly resist sharing marital problems with parents or siblings. This is tempting when you are frustrated or hurting. The problem is that after you resolve the conflict, your family will still remember the hurt your spouse caused you even after you've long forgotten it. These situations can cause great misunderstanding and drive a wedge into family relationships that can be difficult to repair.

4. How would you rate your relationship with your future in-laws on a scale of 1 to 10 (10 being best)? Explain.

If you rate the relationship as a 10, there is only one direction for it to go. Give the relationship room and time to grow. If you rate the relationship low, remember that negative talk about your in-laws can still be very hurtful to your fiancé (even if it is true). When relationships get off to a challenging beginning, they can still get better over time if you continue to respond in love. Don't be controlled by their response but love them where they are because that is what God calls you to do.

A good thing to remember is that your parents will be much more understanding of you than of your spouse. If you have negative news to deliver to your parents, such as, "We will not be able to attend a family event with you because we have another commitment," you should each make sure that you deliver the news to your parents. Conversely, whenever you have an opportunity to deliver good news, try to be the one to tell your in-laws. This will help create a positive relationship with the in-laws.

5. What issues with your extended family might create a strain on your marriage?

Extended family can be a source of friction between couples. The most crucial objective is that you and your fiancé maintain a united front when dealing with family. Discuss problems together. Show compassion for your partner's struggles. Pray together for a good resolution. Draw on the strength of the Holy Spirit to give you a united attitude toward your family, and then family challenges will not tear you apart but will strengthen you.

6. Describe in detail where and with whom you will spend your first Thanksgiving and Christmas.

You may not be able to spend equal time with both families each year. If this is sensitive, look to make it as fair as you can over the years.

7. What can you do to express your love to your parents and future in-laws?

You might want to write them a note or take them out with the specific intention of expressing that you are looking forward to having them as in-laws and that you are thankful to them for giving you such a wonderful fiancé. You could also write a note to your parents and give it to them right before the wedding, thanking them and telling them how much you love them. One more thing you can do for your parents and in-laws is always to keep them in your prayers.

 DO YOU HAVE ANY QUESTIONS ABOUT CHAPTER TEN?

Chapter 11

COMMUNICATION

Do not let any unwholesome talk come out of your mouths,
but only what is helpful for building others up according to their needs,
that it may benefit those who listen — Ephesians 4:29

1. Which of the communication styles below describe your fiancé? Mark all that apply.

CHECK ALL THAT APPLY
Communicates with lack of detail
Communicates with excessive detail
Communicates with a loud or angry voice
Fails to communicate things that I should know; for example, does not tell me about an upcoming social engagement until days after they knew about it
Often does not communicate what they are really thinking
Often becomes defensive when discussing things
Communicates intentionally hurtful things
Retreats and stops communicating at all
Other

Do you agree with the observations your partner made about areas of communication that need some growth in your relationship? The first step towards correcting a problem is acknowledging your role in it. Once the communication shortcoming is identified, you can agree as a couple to nicely point out when your partner slips into a negative communication pattern. Agree in advance that when your partner does this, you will attempt to correct the problem without being defensive so you can work towards building healthier communication habits.

2. On a scale of 1 to 10, ten being best, how would you rate your partner's listening skills?

Few skills are more critical in a marriage than listening. Skilled listeners focus on what is being said rather than thinking about how they will respond to what is being said. James 1:19 emphasizes, "...take note of this: Everyone should be quick to listen, slow to speak and slow to become angry."

Sometimes, it isn't so much that you aren't being heard but that you aren't being understood. Reflective listening (asking your partner to repeat back what they just heard you say) is an excellent way to make sure that you are being understood.

Another excellent way to enable your words to penetrate your partner's heart so that they truly understand and feel your words' impact is to use emotional word pictures. To learn more about this communication tool, read *The Language of Love* by Gary Smalley and John Trent.

3. Does your fiancé interrupt you? If yes, how does it make you feel?

Some women converse in an interactive listening style that can be interpreted as interrupting, but this is not meant to be disrespectful. If this is an issue in your communication, the woman should understand that her guy might be frustrated by it. Likewise, a man should realize that this is not meant to be disrespectful. Be patient and understanding with one another. This typically only becomes a problem when you are not dwelling in your sweet spot. Try to resolve the core problem that has pulled you into the sour patch.

4. How often does your fiancé criticize you?

Excessive criticism is one of the most common destroyers of relationships. Most of us are aware of how often we are criticized, but we are seldom aware of how often we criticize.

When you are tempted to criticize, affirm instead, and you will soon see a significant change in your relationship.

WHEN YOU RECEIVE CRITICISM, THERE ARE THREE BASIC WAYS TO RECEIVE IT:

A) You can deeply resent the criticism. This allows your hurt to turn to poison in your heart, which ultimately hurts you, not the other person.

B) You can lash out towards your partner. However, this just escalates things in a negative direction. If you are right, no defense is necessary. If you are wrong, no defense will do.

C) You can receive the lesson and release the lesion. Although criticism by nature may sting, there can be an element of truth to what is being said. Therefore, evaluate the criticism to receive any constructive criticism and release any hurt to God.

Many proverbs address that the wise welcome criticism, rebuke, and reproof, but fools hate and reject it. If you have trouble with criticism, a good homework assignment would be to read one chapter of Proverbs a day for a month, matching the chapter number to the day of the month. Remember that God is love, love is kind, and God rebukes, so not all rebukes are unkind.

5. Give an example of when your fiancé was brutally honest instead of lovingly honest with you. How could they have communicated better in that situation?

When you are lovingly honest, you are giving honesty in a loving way. When you are brutally honest, you deliver honesty in a manner meant to hurt.

Before you speak, stop and THINK. Ask yourself if what you are about to say is True, Helpful, Inspiring, Necessary, and Kind. If you cannot answer yes to these, then hold your thought.

If you are anxious to confront a situation and cannot do it in a kind way, then perhaps it is not the right time. Instead, allow yourself time to gather your thoughts to speak the truth with love and kindness. Brutal honesty is never appropriate.

6. When you are in the sweet spot in your relationship, do you still experience communication problems?

Couples experiencing difficulty in their relationship often express that they are having communication problems. The truth is that faulty communication is usually not the problem but a symptom of a problem or problems. However, improving your communication skills can often be the first step towards addressing the real issue. In the next chapter, we will learn skills to resolve the core problem.

 **DO YOU HAVE ANY QUESTIONS ABOUT CHAPTER ELEVEN?**

Chapter 12

RESOLVING CONFLICT

When a man's ways are pleasing to the LORD,
he makes even his enemies live at peace with him — Proverbs 16:7

---

1. What is the difference between a discussion and an argument?

In an argument, the parties try to prove who is right, whereas, in a discussion, they try to determine what is right. In an argument, there is competition. In a discussion, there is collaboration.

A sure way to turn a discussion into an argument is to criticize or attack personally. The best ways to turn an argument into a discussion are to begin acknowledging areas where you agree with the other person so you can start collaborating or setting a time in the future to discuss the problem so that emotions can cool down. The keys are to avoid escalating discussions and calm arguments into discussions.

Refer to Appendix 6 in your workbook to review the "Rules for Discussion." Having sound rules for discussions will help minimize arguments.

MENTOR NOTE

Appendix 6 from the workbook appears on the next page.

 **ANY QUESTIONS ON THE RULES FOR DISCUSSION? WORK ON INCORPORATING THESE RULES INTO YOUR EVERYDAY CONVERSATIONS.**

RULES FOR DISCUSSION

1. Speak in a quiet voice.

2. Do not interrupt.

3. Do not bring up the past.

4. Do not blame.

5. Do not use profanity.

6. Do not criticize.

7. Use "I feel" statements, not attacking "you" statements.

8. State your feelings, not your partner's.

9. Never threaten your relationship.

 **ANY QUESTIONS ON THE RULES FOR DISCUSSION? WORK ON INCORPORATING THESE RULES INTO YOUR EVERYDAY CONVERSATIONS.**

2. Name one or more minor conflicts in your relationship that do not need to be resolved (a minor conflict is a disagreement that does not cause harm to the relationship or a conflict that will go away on its own).

Minor conflicts do not need to be formally resolved. Anything that does not continue to drive a wedge into your relationship is a small conflict. Minor disagreements can usually be settled through compromise. For instance, suppose you want to go out to dinner but disagree on where to go. One of you might pick three possibilities from which the other chooses. Or you might alternate who picks each time.

3. List one or more moderate conflicts in your relationship (a moderate conflict is a conflict that does not threaten a healthy relationship, but its resolution would generate more harmony).

An excellent tool to resolve a moderate conflict is to use the practice of *Start or Stop and Continue*. The bothered partner starts by wisely choosing a time when they are both rested and can peacefully discuss the issue. Then this person lovingly explains the problem and asks the other person to either start the desired action or stop the unwanted action. They follow up by sharing something good they would like the partner to continue doing. Basically, the hurt partner is lovingly giving constructive criticism at the right time, followed by a nice affirmation. This is a sure way to resolve a moderate conflict. Remember to follow the "Rules for Discussions" discussed in Appendix 6.

4. List one or more major conflicts in your relationship (a major conflict is a significant issue that, if left unresolved, would damage or threaten a healthy relationship; or a recurring dispute that continually causes dissension).

Refer to Appendix 7 in your workbook, "Ten Rules to Resolve Conflict." This is a time-tested, highly effective method for resolving conflict in a relationship. Let's take a close look at the "Ten Rules to Resolve Conflict."

MENTOR NOTE

Appendix 7 from the workbook appears on the next page.

TEN RULES TO RESOLVE CONFLICT

1. Define the issue to be resolved.

2. Set a time to meet.

3. Set a private place to meet.

4. Begin in prayer.

5. Each share your position.

6. Each point out what you have done to contribute to the problem.

7. Each point out what you can do to help resolve the issue.

8. Agree on a resolution acceptable to both.

9. Write down the resolution.

10. End in prayer.

HERE ARE A FEW FINAL POINTERS BEFORE RESOLVING A CONFLICT

• Be sure to set the conflict resolution for a later time. This allows emotions to settle and provides an opportunity for both of you to think about what you want to say.

• Each of you should open in prayer. If you are uncomfortable with prayer, the prayer can be as simple as, "Please, God, be with us."

• Face each other and hold hands.

• Be sure to both complete each step before going on to the next one.

• Remember to refer to the "Ten Rules to Resolve Conflict" as often as you need to so that you don't accidentally skip a step.

• When you agree on your actions to achieve your resolution, write them down and put them in a prominent place. Then, refer to them daily to stay focused and committed to your solution.

 ## DO YOU HAVE ANY QUESTIONS ABOUT CHAPTER TWELVE?

 ## CLOSING COMMENTS

• Set up a time for your next session.

• If your couple cited a major conflict when answering question 4, request that they set up time before the next session to follow the model in Appendix 7, "Ten Rules to Resolve Conflict," and to come prepared to share the results at their next session.

• Close in prayer.

Before You Meet

By now, your couple will most likely be very comfortable sharing with you. Even so, your couple may be reluctant to share their deepest thoughts on emotional intimacy, especially the couples who need this chapter the most.

HERE ARE SOME ADDITIONAL TIPS:

- If you suspect your couple is avoiding sharing at a deep level, give them additional time to answer. Don't be afraid to allow for times of silence. You can also ask follow-up questions to help them open up. Remember, the success of the mentoring is based on their willingness to communicate openly and honestly with each other.

- Sometimes couples want to compromise on some of the affair-proofing principles presented in this session. Don't let your couple compromise when it comes to understanding these concepts.

- Each week it is important that you read the mentor's notes for each of the three chapters so you understand each question's purpose in the chapter. In addition, it is essential for you to be familiar with the chapter content in the couple's workbook for the three chapters you will be covering during the session.

Chapter 13

EMOTIONAL INTIMACY

Two are better than one — Ecclesiastes 4:9

 ASK YOUR COUPLE HOW THEY DID WITH RESOLVING THEIR CONFLICT.

 ASK YOUR COUPLE IF THEY PRAYED TOGETHER THIS WEEK.

 ASK YOUR COUPLE IF THEY COMPLETED THE KING/QUEEN FOR THE DAY AGAIN THIS WEEK.

 ASK YOUR COUPLE IF THEY HAVE BEEN FAITHFUL TO THEIR PREMARITAL COVENANT.

1. On a scale of 1 to 10 (10 being best), rate the accuracy of the following statements.

STATEMENT	RATING
I feel emotionally connected and understood by my fiancé. If you do not feel connected, what would make you feel connected?	
I feel comfortable and safe sharing my deepest thoughts and feelings with my fiancé. If you're uncomfortable sharing your deepest thoughts, what do you fear?	
I trust my fiancé to keep my confidences. If trust is missing, what can your fiancé do to begin rebuilding trust? You need to give your partner a way to win.	
I feel my fiancé knows me better than any other person. If you do not feel you know each other, spend some special time sharing your dreams.	

I believe we will make important decisions together as a team in marriage. God wants you to operate as a team—two becoming one. You cannot experience emotional intimacy if you are not a team. Two heads are always better than one.	
In marriage, I believe we will hold each other accountable in a God-honoring way. If you see a correction your fiancé needs, do it privately and gently. Always affirm your belief that they can make the needed correction. Also, be receptive to receiving corrections from your partner. Take personal responsibility for your failures. Do not defend or make excuses. Instead, thank your fiancé for pointing them out.	
We pray together as a couple on a regular basis. Praying together regularly at a deep, heartfelt level creates a spiritual bonding. So what is standing in the way of this taking place?	

2. What is the biggest deterrent to being more vulnerable with your fiancé (such as fear of trusting, rejection, judgment, losing control, appearing weak, or getting a negative response)?

The imprint from our family of origin shapes our behaviors, beliefs, and expectations of all relationships, especially our marriages. Consider how your early experiences of care and comfort (or lack of care and comfort)—especially from your parents—have shaped your ability and desire for connection and closeness. Hurts and traumas from our past cause fear or make it hard to trust others. If these hurts impede emotional intimacy with your fiancé, you may need to get some additional help to heal those wounds.

3. Do you see any negative behaviors hindering emotional intimacy in your relationship (such as avoidance, sarcasm, passive-aggressive behavior, criticism, nagging, anger, self-pity, defensiveness, or family-of-origin imprints)?

You must identify the problem before you can correct it. After you identify the problem, you must want to fix it, make a plan, and then follow the plan. What are some steps you can take to improve this negative behavior pattern?

4. **Technology plays an important role in our lives. Are there any changes you would like to make in your relationship regarding the use of technology that could improve your connectedness as a couple?**

Perhaps you would like your spouse to agree to phone-free mealtimes, or to turning off all devices an hour before bedtime.

Technology can also enhance your connectedness through shared calendars or more frequent messages letting you know where your spouse is or an update on their ETA.

5. **Complete this statement, "This is what I would like you to know about me in order to understand me better …"**

Part of developing a closer relationship and a better understanding of one another is to converse with open and honest communication about your thoughts and feelings.

 DO YOU HAVE ANY QUESTIONS ABOUT CHAPTER THIRTEEN?

Chapter 14

PHYSICAL INTIMACY

I am my lover's and my lover is mine
— Song of Songs 6:3

---

1. Are you comfortable discussing your future sexual needs in marriage with your fiancé?

Open, honest communication is the key to a vibrant sex life. You should be honest about what pleasures you. Mutually satisfying sexual intimacy requires being both selfish and unselfish. Great lovers know their bodies and enjoy their sexual feelings, as well as know and meet the sexual needs of their partner. Remember, you are not mind readers. You need to share with one another honestly. Continue sharing because, especially for women, what feels good one time may not feel that way the next time..

Sharing your needs and wants will not take the romance out of the experience. On the contrary, it allows for better sexual intimacy. The goal should be to combine the best of what you both desire to create a fulfilling love life for both of you. You need to be honest and open with your spouse to experience the sexual fulfillment that God intended you to have in marriage.

2. What concerns or fears do you have concerning sex?

One concern that often comes up with this question is the woman feeling insecure about her looks, no matter how attractive she is. We are bombarded with images of perfect bodies in the media that even the represented models and actors can't live up to after all the airbrushing, etc. This can put a lot of pressure on us to feel like we need to look like the pictures we see in magazines, on billboards, and television. Women, especially, no matter how beautiful they are, tend to feel insecure about their looks. Yet men are visually stimulated and enjoy seeing their wives naked. We need to keep two things in focus. First, God created us the way we are, and we should accept ourselves as we are without comparing ourselves to others. Our fiancé chose us as a partner over billions of others in the world. Second, we should be good stewards of the body God has given us. We need to watch our health, diet, and exercise so that we can always present our best selves to our spouses.

3. What issue or experience from your or your partner's past may affect your intimacy?

People generally don't feel uncomfortable about their past, but they feel insecure about their partner's past. They fear they might be compared. If you feel insecure about past relationships, this can definitely affect your intimacy with your spouse. Share these feelings with your spouse. In talking about past relationships, avoid the details and just work through the issues. Be forgiving of each other and yourself. It is essential to talk openly and honestly.

4. How many times per week do you think you will desire sex in marriage? Your spouse-to-be?

The desire for sexual intimacy within marriage is rarely equal. Our biological differences play into this a great deal. A husband is visual and can become very easily aroused by just seeing his wife's body. He can achieve sexual fulfillment within a few seconds of proper stimulation. A wife's hormones change throughout the month and can affect her sex drive. It takes more effort for her to attain sexual fulfillment. The type and duration of stimulation a wife needs during foreplay can vary significantly from one time to the next.

Never deprive your spouse of your body in love, which is a true gift.

5. What are some creative ways you can keep the romance in your relationship?

After marriage, it is beneficial to continue to let your spouse know that they are still the love of your life by keeping romance alive. Wives especially delight in being sought after and made to feel special. You will feel most amorous when you feel a oneness with your spouse.

The need for romance is not always equal. Even if it is not as necessary for you, wouldn't you always appreciate the effort put into a romantic atmosphere? Wouldn't you enjoy your spouse doing fun, romantic things to make the experience more memorable?

Remember to keep the fun in your sex life. Enjoy each other! Never lose the art of romancing your spouse and making an event out of your lovemaking moments.

 **DO YOU HAVE ANY QUESTIONS ABOUT CHAPTER FOURTEEN?**

Chapter 15

AFFAIR-PROOFING YOUR MARRIAGE

Marriage should be honored by all, and the marriage bed kept pure,
for God will judge the adulterer and all the sexually immoral — Hebrews 13:4

1. In which of the following ways do you engage with friends or work associates of the opposite gender, one-to-one, without the knowledge of your fiancé?

CHECK ALL THAT APPLY
Phone calls
Email
Texting
Commenting on social media
Private messaging through social media
Coffee breaks
Meals/drinks together
Business meetings
Social events

Outside of the workplace, it is never appropriate to carry on a one-to-one, in-depth communication with someone of the opposite sex once you are engaged or married. You should either say no because you are engaged/married, or you should bring your partner into the conversation by cc'ing them or tagging them. Tell your partner about phone conversations that are not work-related. Transparency is key.

Usually, one-to-one social and work situations can be addressed by including a third person. However, if a work situation cannot be avoided, make sure that you meet at an appropriate setting for business, never an intimate setting. Also, take care to keep the conversation on business. Do not allow the conversation to become personal.

2. Is there any relationship that you can identify as needing additional boundaries? What action steps would you suggest putting into place to improve your hedges?

Sometimes your fiancé can intuitively sense when a relationship is getting too close between you and someone of the opposite sex. It may be completely innocent on your part, but the other person may not have such innocent intentions. Or what might be innocent right now has the potential to become inappropriate. So, out of love and respect for your fiancé, take immediate and appropriate action to safeguard your relationship.

3. What is your attitude towards pornography?

Most people in this day and age (especially men) have viewed pornography at some point. Pornography precludes you from enjoying the closeness and intimacy God created for husbands and wives. Pornography is basically a virtual affair. It is like inviting a third party into your bedroom. Even when someone views pornography without the knowledge of their spouse, it will impact their intimacy, often by desensitizing you to your spouse.

Consider these two studies:

> Christians aren't immune. When surveyed, 53% of men who attended Promise Keepers said they viewed pornography that week. More than 45% of Christians admit that pornography is a major problem in their home. An anonymous survey conducted recently by Pastors.com reported that 54% of pastors admitted viewing porn within the last year. In an online newsletter, 34% of female readers of *Today's Christian Woman* admitted to intentionally accessing Internet porn. One out of every six women who read *Today's Christian Woman* say they struggle with addiction to pornography (*Today's Christian Woman*, Fall 2003).[2]

> For the surprising number of husbands who think that pornography use is "no big deal," consider this from those who work at ground zero of divorce. During a recent meeting of divorce attorneys, two-thirds of the 350 attorneys said the Internet played a significant role in the divorces in the past year, with excessive interest in online porn contributing to more than half such cases. Pornography had an almost nonexistent role in divorce just ten or so years ago.[3]

---

[2] Paul Coughlin, "Pornography and Virtual Infidelity," *Focus on the Family*, accessed May 22, 2015, http://www.focusonthefamily.com/marriage/divorce-and-infidelity/pornography-and-virtual-infidelity/virtual-infidelity-and-marriage.

[3] Paul Coughlin, "Erosive Influence of Port Upon Husbands," *Focus on the Family*, accessed May 22, 2015, http://www.focusonthefamily.com/marriage/divorce-and-infidelity/pornography-and-virtual-infidelity/erosive-influence-of-porn-on-husbands.

4. Will you agree to give total access to each other's technology activities?

This is a very healthy and vital safeguard to put in place within your relationship. The key here is transparency and accountability. Share your passwords and keep each other accountable by occasionally checking your partner's history. Not wanting to give access is a red flag.

5. Are you comfortable with the amount of time your fiancé spends away from you? Explain.

Sometimes couples can complacently drift into being like married singles. Make sure your home is a welcoming place for both of you. Greet each other in a loving way when you come together at the end of the day. If your fiancé is engaged in hobbies or outside activities that you can participate in or support as a viewer or fan, be there. If your partner has to work long hours for a season, meet up for a meal or surprise them by bringing them a treat.

6. List five activities or hobbies you enjoy doing together.

Over the years, couples often find that their interests and activities take them in different directions, and they begin to grow apart. So be intentional about continuing to find new ways you enjoy spending time together.

 DO YOU HAVE ANY QUESTIONS ABOUT CHAPTER FIFTEEN?

 AT THIS TIME, THE GUYS ARE GOING TO MEET SEPARATELY IN ANOTHER ROOM WHILE THE LADIES STAY HERE.

MENTOR NOTE

The purpose of separating is threefold.

1. It allows you an opportunity to discuss something you have identified in earlier sessions that you would prefer not to discuss with them as a couple but with just the man or woman.

2. Ask them if they have any questions for you that they want to ask without their partner present.

3. Review "Ten Ways to be a Fantastic Wife/Husband" in Appendices 8 or 9.

Appendices 8 and 9 from the workbook begin on the next page.

Appendix 8

TEN WAYS TO BE A FANTASTIC WIFE

1. Believe in your husband and be his No. 1 fan.

2. Be careful not to nag your husband. Instead, turn over your concerns to God in prayer. Ask God to give you oneness in your marriage.

3. It is not uncommon for a husband to have a greater sex drive than his wife. Take care of his sexual needs.

4. On the first day of each month, put the following question on your calendar: "What must it be like to be married to me?"

5. People tend to be what you say they are. Tell your husband what a great husband, friend, and lover he is. He won't disappoint you.

6. When you come together at the end of the day, greet him in a loving way.

7. Guys are visual; do your best to take care of yourself and be attractive to him.

8. Remember to speak in his love language.

9. Share in his hobbies with him. Continue to be the fun person he married.

10. Put Christ at the center of your life and the center of your marriage.

TEN WAYS TO BE A FANTASTIC HUSBAND

1. Always show your wife how special she is to you.

2. Avoid being too critical. What you may think of as constructive criticism, she may see as an attack on her.

3. If you want to have a great sex life, you must keep some romance in your relationship. Continue to date your wife.

4. On the first day of each month, put the following question on your calendar: "What must it be like to be married to me?"

5. Pray with your wife often. It means more to her than you know.

6. Compliment your wife's appearance. She knows you are visual. So, your compliments are important to her and make her feel special.

7. People tend to be what you say they are. Tell your wife what a great wife, friend, and lover she is. She won't disappoint you.

8. Remember to talk in her love language.

9. Your wife will need to talk. Take time to be a good listener. Often, she won't want a solution; she will just want to talk to you. Value her opinion.

10. Put Christ at the center of your life, your marriage, and be the spiritual leader of your family. Ask your wife how you can be praying for her.

AFTER REVIEWING THE *10 WAYS TO BE A FANTASTIC WIFE/HUSBAND*, THE FOUR OF YOU SHOULD COME BACK TOGETHER TO FINISH THE SESSION.

CLOSING COMMENTS

- Set up a time for your next session.

- Close in prayer.

Before You Meet

As mentors, be sure to finish strong. Some mentors like to conclude by getting together with their couple for a meal. If you choose to do this, we recommend doing it as a seventh meeting, not as part of this sixth session.

HERE ARE SOME ADDITIONAL TIPS:

• Depending on your financial skill level, you may feel comfortable reviewing your couple's *Budget and Financial Statement,* or you may elect to skip this process. At least make sure that they have completed both.

• Unless finance is one of their strengths, strongly encourage them to enroll in a Dave Ramsey or Crown Ministry Workshop. The information for both is in their workbook.

• Each week it is important that you read the mentor's notes for each of the three chapters so you understand each question's purpose in the chapter. In addition, it is essential for you to be familiar with the chapter content in the couple's workbook for the three chapters you will be covering during the session.

• This week ends with a review. You want to make sure that your couple has a good grasp of the concepts and skills introduced throughout the program.

• Write on your calendar to send your couple an encouraging note or email the week of their wedding. Continue to keep them in your prayers.

As you wrap up this final session, recognize that you have just done some incredible work for God. When one marriage improves, it can affect generations to come. May you be blessed for the blessing you have given!

Chapter 16

FINANCES

No servant can serve two masters. Either he will hate the one and love the other,
or he will be devoted to the one and despise the other.
You cannot serve God and Money — Luke 16:13

 ASK YOUR COUPLE IF THEY PRAYED TOGETHER THIS WEEK.

 ASK YOUR COUPLE IF THEY COMPLETED THE KING/QUEEN FOR THE DAY AGAIN THIS WEEK.

 ASK YOUR COUPLE IF THEY HAVE BEEN FAITHFUL TO THEIR PREMARITAL COVENANT.

1. On a scale of 1 to 10 (10 being best), how good is your ability to manage money?

If you are below a 6 or 7, you should seek additional financial guidance. Two excellent resources given in your workbook are www.DaveRamsey.com and www.crown.org. You might also benefit from reading Dave Ramsey's book, *The Total Money Makeover.*

2. Will you have joint accounts, separate accounts, or both?

There is no right or wrong to this. The main thing is that you discuss it and agree upon it. Transparency with your income and spending is critical. Using a free tool like https://mint.intuit.com is a great way to ensure transparency with your money matters. Once you set it up, it will give you an up-to-the-minute overview of your finances. You can also set up a budget on this program to keep track of your progress.

3. Which one of you will pay the bills? Why?

Whichever one of you is most responsible should be the one who ultimately makes sure that the bills are paid every month. However, finances should be a team effort. Plan a time every month to sit down together as a team to review your budget. Both of you should be fully aware of your financial situation.

4. Fill in the blank. I think any _discretionary_ purchase over the following amount should require the agreement of both the husband and the wife:

$ _____

The amount is not as important as the ability for both to agree on the amount. One thing to keep in mind is that you will value things differently. For example, one of you may put a high value on buying clothes. The other one may place more value on buying computer games.

Remember that discretionary spending is not for necessities. It is optional, fun spending with extra money after your obligations are met. You will probably have different ways you will want to spend your extra money.

5. Identify an area where your fiancé spends money for which you don't understand the value or importance.

A wife may have trouble understanding why her husband spends $100 on a computer game. Likewise, a husband may not understand why his wife spends $100 on a purse. Neither one of these is wrong, provided you can afford the purchases. It is essential to make purchases that are within budget and not impulsive. Recognize that you will likely have different ways you will each want to spend discretionary income. Provided it fits into your budget, be understanding of your differences.

6. If you received unexpected cash of $100,000, how do you recommend spending it as a couple?

7. What do you believe your current FICO score is? Your partner's?

FICO scores range between 350 and 850. An average FICO score is around 680, and anything above 720 is considered excellent. If you are unaware of your current FICO score, you can obtain it online for free at www.CreditKarma.com. Your FICO score is a good indicator of how well you manage your finances and plays a big part in obtaining financing for big purchases such as a home. Always paying your bills on time and not maximizing your credit lines are two key factors in achieving a good score.

8. What is your biggest concern for your future finances as a couple?

9. Complete an Annual Budget and a Financial Statement of Net Worth together with your fiancé. You can use the guides on the following pages to assist you.

MENTOR NOTE

Make sure that your couple completed their "Monthly Budget" and "Financial Statement of Worth" together. Depending on your financial abilities, you may feel comfortable reviewing these forms with your couple, or you may prefer to limit your comments. Encourage your couple to continue being a student of finances by enrolling in either a Dave Ramsey class or a Crown Ministries course. These are often offered at local churches.

DO YOU HAVE QUESTIONS ABOUT CHAPTER SIXTEEN?

Chapter 17

MARRIAGE GOALS

Commit to the LORD whatever you do,
and your plans will succeed — Proverbs 16:3

---

1. What Bible verse would you like to commit to memory this year? This verse should focus on helping you improve one area in your life.

Imagine how much personal improvement will occur if you memorize a new verse each year.

2. List some of your ideas for goals in the following areas:

TYPE OF GOAL / GOAL IDEAS
Spiritual
Time with each other
Family

TYPE OF GOAL / GOAL IDEAS	
Vacation	You will likely be going on a honeymoon your first year. It is valuable to schedule vacation time together every year. Remember, you don't have to leave town to have a vacation.
Personal	
Health and fitness	Commit to taking good care of your health as a gift to your partner.

3. **Make a date with your fiancé to develop goals as a couple for the year.**
   Write the specific date, time, and place below.

 DO YOU HAVE ANY QUESTIONS ABOUT CHAPTER SEVENTEEN?

Chapter 18

KEEPING THE FLAME GOING

The fear of the LORD is the beginning of wisdom,
and knowledge of the Holy One is understanding — Proverbs 9:10

MENTOR NOTE

The twenty-one questions and explanations from the workbook begin below. For the questions your couple answered for Chapter 18, the questions immediately follow.

TWENTY-ONE QUESTIONS

1. ARE ALL THREE TYPES OF LOVE (EROS, PHILIA, AND AGAPE) PRESENT IN YOUR MARRIAGE?

Review the list you wrote of ten things you love about your fiancé in Chapter 2. Discuss together how you can each express the three types of love towards each other more fully. Keep this list available and refer to it often. Whenever you become discouraged about your marriage, reread the list of things you love about your partner. One of the most effective tools for overcoming marital disappointment is replacing a negative thought about your husband or wife with thoughts of gratitude. Studies show that we can focus on only one emotion at a time: choose love. (Refer to Chapter 2.)

2. HAVE YOU BOTH FORGIVEN EACH OTHER FOR EVERYTHING?

Make sure forgiveness flows freely between you and your spouse for BIG and small conflicts. Practice forgiving, not collecting, hurts. God has forgiven us for all our sins. He wants us to forgive one another freely. "Bear with each other and forgive whatever grievances you may have against one another. Forgive as the Lord forgave you" (Colossians 3:13). We forgive by faith, out of obedience to God. God wants us to love others and to love Him. This love He speaks of is a choice, not a feeling. We must trust God to complete His work in us. Make it between you and God and not between you and your spouse. Turn your heart over to God. Corrie ten Boom, a Christian who survived a Nazi concentration camp, said, "Forgiveness is the key that unlocks the door of resentment and the handcuffs of hatred. It is a power that breaks the chains of bitterness and the shackles of selfishness."[4] One of the most loving actions you can continually take is forgiving. (Refer to Chapter 3.)

---

[4] Corrie ten Boom, *Clippings from My Notebook* (Nashville: Thomas Nelson, 1982), pg 19.

3. ARE YOU LIVING OUT THE BIBLICAL ROLES OUTLINED FOR A HUSBAND AND WIFE IN EPHESIANS 5:21–33?

We each need to worshipfully surrender our lives to Christ. Ultimately, a wife answers to God for how well she submits to her husband's leadership, whether or not he is making good, loving decisions. Ultimately, a husband answers to God for how well he loves his wife, regardless of whether or not she respects and submits to him.

When your spouse falls short of living out God's will in your marriage, take your frustrations to God. Trust God to meet your needs, and He will fill you with His love to take back to the marriage. In doing this, instead of expecting perfect behavior from two imperfect people, you look for the perfect response from your perfect God. (Refer to Chapter 4.)

4. ARE YOU CONTINUING TO PRAY TOGETHER OFTEN?

If not, start by setting a time at least once a week to pray together. Remember, God wants to bless your marriage beyond your imagination, but you need to invite Him in and follow His will together. There is nothing more important than keeping God at the center of your marriage. (Refer to Chapter 4.)

5. DO YOU CONTINUE TO SHARE SPECIFICALLY WITH YOUR SPOUSE HOW THEY CAN PRAY FOR YOU?

Prayer is one of the most loving, intimate expressions that can be exchanged between a husband and wife. After you share your prayer requests, pray out loud together for each other. (Refer to Chapter 4.)

6. IS YOUR SPOUSE MEETING YOUR MOST IMPORTANT WANTS AND NEEDS?

You may desire a weekly date night; time to talk about light topics; fun together doing a hobby; more frequent sex; more transparency with the finances; more home cooking; being more physically active; entertaining more (or less) with family and friends; hearing more affirming statements; having more intimate, open, honest conversations; etc. Lovingly share your desires with your spouse.

We should not look to our spouse to make us happy. There will be times in your marriage when it will be more profitable to take the focus off your partner meeting your wants and put your focus on God. Philippians 4:19 assures us, "God will meet all your needs according to His glorious riches in Christ Jesus." Bob and Judy Hughes' book, *Love Focused,* is an excellent resource to understand this concept better. They also have a couples Bible study you could do together. (Refer to Chapter 5.)

7. HAVE YOU ESTABLISHED A WEEKLY KING FOR THE DAY AND QUEEN FOR THE DAY?

Share with each other what you would like your spouse to do for you on your day. Be attentive to meeting your spouse's wishes on their day. Remember, this can be a real game changer. (Refer to Chapter 5.)

8. ARE THERE ANY AREAS IN WHICH YOU FEEL YOUR SPOUSE IS NOT SUCCESSFULLY FULFILLING THEIR ROLE IN MARRIAGE?

God gives specific instructions for husbands to love their wives as Christ loved the church. God instructs wives to respect their husbands and submit to their leadership in the family. This does not mean that a husband controls all areas of marriage. Instead, a godly leader recognizes the best gifted in given areas and gives jurisdiction for those responsibilities to the best-qualified person. Lovingly discuss any roles you would like to see changed or improved, and share what betterment looks like to you. (Refer to Chapter 5.)

9. ARE YOU SPENDING MOST OF YOUR TIME IN THE SWEET SPOT?

A marriage has momentum in the direction of the sweet spot or the sour patch. If you are not spending most of your time in the sweet spot, go back and review the eighteen skills for staying in the sweet spot. Remember, fun is the litmus test of a good relationship. Do something fun together. (Refer to Chapter 6.)

10. ARE YOU DEALING EFFECTIVELY WITH YOUR INCOMPATIBILITIES?

A great marriage is not based on marrying someone compatible because God does not make any two people perfectly compatible; it is based on learning how to deal effectively with your incompatibilities. If you are struggling with compatibility, consider taking a Myers-Briggs Type Indicator® instrument to identify your personality styles (http://www.16personalities.com offers a free test online). Remember, there is no right or wrong to personality differences. You are both created in the image of God. Work on becoming more understanding and accepting of the fact that you approach life differently. (Refer to Chapter 7.)

11. ARE THE DIFFERENCES BETWEEN MEN AND WOMEN CAUSING FRICTION IN YOUR MARRIAGE?

Men and women have very different operating systems. We will never completely understand each other, but we can educate ourselves on what is important to each other. The book *Love and Respect* by Emerson Eggerrichs gives a deeper understanding of our differences. You may want to consider reading the book together. Ultimately, God wants our differences to complement and complete each other in marriage as we work together as one. (Refer to Chapter 8.)

12. HOW FULL IS YOUR LOVE TANK ON A SCALE OF 1 TO 10? WHAT CAN YOUR SPOUSE DO TO MAKE IT A 10?

Remember to speak to your spouse in their love language and remind your spouse to talk to you in your language. In addition, you may want to read the book, *The Five Love Languages* by Gary Chapman. (Refer to Chapter 9.)

13. ARE THERE ANY ISSUES WITH YOUR FAMILY RELATIONSHIPS CAUSING PROBLEMS IN YOUR MARRIAGE?

Discuss what you can do to improve any family tension. Be sure that your relationship with each other is kept primary and that you always show a united front. When problems arise with your family, face them together. Discuss them together as husband and wife. Pray about them together. If needed, seek outside counsel from trusted advisors or professionals. With kids, keep things in perspective. Don't major in minors. If it is not life-altering for your child, natural consequences may be the best teacher. If extended family members are causing issues, sometimes it is best to set healthy boundaries to protect your primary family relationships. (Refer to Chapter 10.)

14. ARE YOU COMMUNICATING WITH EACH OTHER EFFECTIVELY?

Content, tone, and body language are all essential aspects of communication but listening and choosing the appropriate time for sensitive conversations are also important. Work on any weaknesses in your communication. When couples have trouble with communication, it is often a symptom of a bigger issue. Try to identify the more significant problem and work that through using the tools offered through this program such as the "Ten Rules to Resolve Conflict" in Appendix 7. Above all, always speak to each other in love using the "Rules for Discussion" in Appendix 6. (Refer to Chapter 11.)

15. DO YOU HAVE ANY UNRESOLVED CONFLICTS IN YOUR MARRIAGE?

Conflicts come in all shapes and sizes. With moderate disputes, use the *Start or Stop and Continue Method*. Also, holding your spouse's hand and praying together can often soften hearts to restore peace. However, if you have a major conflict, set a time to use the "Ten Rules to Resolve Conflict" in Appendix 7 to resolve your dispute. (Refer to Chapter 12.)

16. ARE YOU ENJOYING THE EMOTIONAL INTIMACY YOU DESIRE WITH YOUR SPOUSE?

You should feel comfortable and safe sharing your most intimate thoughts and dreams with each other. It is as if you are saying, "into-me-see." Growing in this area involves continual effort and investment in your relationship. (Refer to Chapter 13.)

17. DO YOU HAVE A VIBRANT SEX LIFE?

If your love life isn't all that you would like it to be, the best way to revitalize your physical intimacy is to communicate openly and honestly with each other. Truthfully communicate your desires to your spouse. Be sensitive and loving in fulfilling your partner's wishes. Try something fun like showering together. (Refer to Chapter 14.)

18. IS YOUR MARRIAGE SAFELY AFFAIR-PROOFED?

It's too late to prevent an affair after it's happened. Protect your marriage by keeping proper boundaries in place. It is imperative that you give each other full access to all your communication devices and social networking sites. Discuss if there are any areas that need to be reinforced. (Refer to Chapter 15.)

19. ARE YOUR FINANCES HEALTHY?

Be transparent with each other with your spending. Recognize that you will likely have different ways you will each want to spend discretionary income. Provided it fits into your budget, be understanding of your differences. A budget and financial statement are good ways to keep track of your finances. A helpful tool for creating a budget and maintaining transparency with your finances is https://www.mint.intuit.com. If you need some extra guidance on your finances, many churches offer financial counseling following either Dave Ramsey's principles or Crown Ministries. Find information on these programs at www.daveramsey.com and www.crown.org. (Refer to Chapter 16.)

20. HAVE YOU SET GOALS TOGETHER AS A COUPLE?

One of the cornerstones of this program is having an intentional marriage. Relationships are either getting better or getting worse. They don't stay the same. Therefore, it is important to continue pursuing goals and dreams as a couple. For this to happen, you need to set goals and take action steps. In order for goals to truly take hold, they should be written down and reviewed for progress. (Refer to Chapter 17.)

21. ARE YOU INVOLVED IN A SMALL GROUP FOR COUPLES?

Fellowship with other believers is one of the conduits God uses to share His truth with us. Communing with other Christian married couples will help enrich your marriage through shared life experiences and godly insights. (Refer to Chapter 17.)

1. In taking inventory on your relationship today using the questions above, which areas did you identify as still needing growth? Be honest. Please list the numbers of those questions.

2. Decide the dates for your quarterly marriage assessment and tune-up. Write the dates below.

3. Turn back to page 15 and read your answer to question 2 (Chapter 1). How well did you achieve what your were hoping to accomplish through this program?

DO YOU HAVE ANY QUESTIONS ABOUT CHAPTER EIGHTEEN?

CLOSING COMMENTS

- Your premarital mentoring is now complete. This program was designed to give you God's blueprint so you would know the actions to take to experience a joyful marriage. You will need to make a commitment to continue investing in your relationship intentionally. One final comment: remember to keep the main thing, the main thing. What is the main thing? **Keep Christ at the center of your marriage.**

- All hold hands and pray out loud together. We suggest designating that the male mentor will close out the prayer.